Primary Symbols of Worship

And the Call to Participation

Mary Amore

Resource Publications, Inc.
San Jose, California

© 2004 Resource Publications, Inc. All rights reserved. No part of this book may be photocopied or otherwise reproduced without permission from the publisher. For reprint permission, contact:

Reprint Department
Resource Publications, Inc.
160 E. Virginia St. #290
San Jose, CA 95112-5876
(408) 286-8505
(408) 287-8748 fax

Library of Congress Cataloging-in-Publications Data
Amore, Mary, 1952-
    Primary symbols of worship : and the call to participation / by Mary Amore.
       p. cm.
    ISBN 0-89390-607-7
    1. Worship. 2. Catholic Church—Liturgy. 3. Catholic Church—Doctrines. I. Title.
    BX1969.A66 2004
    264'.02—dc22

                                                                                                       2004041757

Printed in the United States of America
04 05 06 07 08 | 5 4 3 2 1

Production Staff: Nelson Estarija, Laura Quilling, Susan Carter
Back cover photo: Don Box

Excerpts from the New American Bible with Revised New Testament and Psalms Copyright © 1991, 1986, 1970 Confraternity of Christian Doctrine, Inc., Washington, DC. Used with permission. All rights reserved. No portion of the New American Bible may be reprinted without permission in writing from the copyright holder.

Excerpts from Built of Living Stones © 2000 United States Conference of Catholic Bishops, Inc., Washington, DC. Used with permission. All rights reserved. No part of the text may be reproduced by any means without permission in writing from the copyright holder.

Excerpts from the English translation of the Introduction to the *Lectionary for Mass* © 1981, International Committee on English in the Liturgy, Inc. (ICEL); excerpts from the English translation of the General Introduction to the *Rite of Christian Initiation of Adults* © 1985, ICEL; excerpts from the English translation of the *General Instruction of the Roman Missal* © 2002, ICEL. All rights reserved.

I lovingly dedicate this book to my family:

Joe, Lauren, and Joey,

who encouraged me on this journey,

and to

Father Scott McCawley,

who helped me take the first step.

Contents

List of Abbreviations. vii

Introduction. 1

Chapter One
The Evolutionary Church:
Our Roots and Our Future. 5

Chapter Two
The Waters of Baptism:
Doorway to New Life and Call to Community. 11

Chapter Three
The Ambo: Altar of the Living Word 17

Chapter Four
The Altar: Table of Transformation 23

Chapter Five
The Worshiping Assembly:
The Living Body of Christ 29

Chapter Six
The Pilgrim Church: Sacred Space in Transition. 35

Bibliography 40

List of Abbreviations

BLS	*Built of Living Stones: Art, Architecture, and Worship*
CCC	*Catechism of the Catholic Church*
CSL	*Constitution on the Sacred Liturgy*
FIYH	*Fulfilled in Your Hearing*
GIRM	*General Instruction of the Roman Missal*
LM	*Lectionary for Mass*
RCIA	*Rite of Christian Initiation of Adults*
RCIA GI	*Rite of Christian Initiation of Adults,* "Christian Initiation, General Introduction"
RDCA	*Rite of Dedication of a Church and an Altar*
UR	*Unitatis redintegratio:* Vatican Council II, Decree on Ecumenism

Introduction

On December 4, 1963, the bishops of the Second Vatican Council promulgated the *Constitution on the Sacred Liturgy* and instituted renewal of the sacred liturgy:

> In the reform and promotion of the liturgy, this full and active participation by all the people is the aim to be considered before all else. For it is the primary and indispensable source from which the faithful are to derive the true Christian spirit (14).

For Roman Catholics of the twentieth century, this profound proclamation would be a watershed in the liturgical life of the church, for it would alter the ecclesiology of the assembly.

In the decades that followed the Second Vatican Council, a considerable amount of time and effort has been spent nurturing this call to active participation on behalf of the laity. From catechizing the people on their roles as ministers of the assembly to diligently recruiting and training people for various liturgical ministries, parishes everywhere have worked in the spirit of Vatican II to bring about full and active participation for all believers. As both a member of the assembly and a full-time director of liturgy, my experiences working with laity and clergy have taught me that our task is far from complete!

The Birth of this Book

The concept for this book came from my experience as the liturgical advisor for the renovation project of my home parish, St. Mary of Gostyn in Downers Grove, Illinois. It became evident that our vibrant, spirit-filled faith community needed liturgical catechesis to help them make a connection between their worship experience and the primary symbols of the rituals that shape our lives as Catholics. I began a yearlong series of bulletin articles, adult faith formation talks, town hall meetings, and small group discussions, which focused on helping the parish gain a deeper insight into the intimate relationship between the assembly's call to participation in the liturgy and *the primary symbols of worship*.

Focusing on the liturgical rituals of baptizing, proclaiming, feasting, and commissioning as primary liturgical actions of the Christian community at prayer, we studied the following questions:

- What is our experience of the life-giving waters of baptism?

- How is baptism intimately linked to the celebration of Eucharist?

- In what ways does the word of God work within us and prepare us for mission?

- In what manner are the Liturgy of the Word and the Liturgy of the Eucharist connected?

- How are we transformed at the eucharistic banquet?

- As disciples of Christ, in what ways are we called to be the Body and Blood of Christ in the world?

- How do we gather for prayers as a faith community?

- How do we welcome the strangers in our midst?

The results of our discussions led us to focus on the primary symbols of worship: *the font, the ambo, the altar table,* and *the assembly* and how these symbols engage our spiritual imagination and active participation in the liturgical life of the church. Over time, the parish family of St. Mary's grew in spiritual awareness of the nature of these powerful liturgical symbols and how these symbols call forth their full, conscious, and active participation in the saving mission of Jesus Christ.

Using This Book

This book is for the primary ministers of liturgical celebrations: the baptized faithful. It is a pastoral resource intended to catechize each of the primary symbols of worship and how these symbols influence the community's call to active participation through theological and liturgical insights. The opening chapter offers a glimpse into the history of Roman

Catholic Christian worship and the effects thereof of the liturgical renewal brought about by the Second Vatican Council. Chapter Two looks at the communal call to active participation rooted in the sacrament of baptism. In Chapter Three we examine the assembly's communal call to active participation, rooted in God's word. Chapter Four covers the community's call to active participation in the eucharistic banquet and mission work of Christ. In Chapter Five we continue with the important work of the assembly actively accepting the invitation to communal worship as the living Body of Christ. Chapter Six offers insight into how we claim nontraditional, temporary worship settings for full and active worship experiences. Discussion questions at the end of each chapter are useful for personal study and for parish gatherings, small groups, and families. Also included are guided meditations, which are experiential in nature and intended to enhance liturgical spirituality.

A Word of Thanks

I'd like to express my heartfelt gratitude to Reverend Thomas Paul, pastor of St. Mary of Gostyn Parish, for sharing his wisdom and knowledge and the people of St. Mary's, who taught me the true meaning of church and who have been a continual source of inspiration and support during this project. Most importantly, I am immensely grateful to my husband, Joe, and my two teenage children, Lauren and Joey, for their enduring love, patience, and understanding during the writing of this book.

Chapter One

The Evolutionary Church: Our Roots and Our Future

Since the beginning of Christianity, the role of the assembly at worship has undergone many transitions, some of which have enhanced the participation of the people at worship and some that have hindered it. In the early days of the church, the faithful gathered in private homes (*the domus ecclesiae*) to break bread. These early eucharistic meals centered on the family table, a symbol of fellowship and love in ancient times. St. Luke describes the milieu of these early Christian gatherings:

> Every day they devoted themselves to meeting together in the temple area and to breaking bread in their homes. They ate their meals with exultation and sincerity of heart, praising God and enjoying favor with all the people (Acts 2:46–47).

Despite fear from persecution, the early Christians continued to enjoy the intimate setting of breaking bread in local house churches for the first centuries of Christianity. In 380 A.D. the Constantine Empire proclaimed Christianity the official religion. This imperial declaration had a staggering effect on the ancient Christian community and the manner in which the faithful gathered for worship. With Christianity now the official religion of the empire, the population of baptized Christians saw a dramatic rise. As a result, the worship setting of the domestic church no longer accommodated the worshiping needs of the rapidly growing Christian community, which also included members of the royal courts. Larger and more majestic structures to house the growing number of Christians gave rise to the birth of the Christian basilica.

These enormous houses of prayer, patterned after secular Roman basilicas, were massive stone buildings characterized by a long rectangular room with an apse, a semicircular room projecting from the end wall at the far end. The apse housed the bishop's chair (*Cathedra*), and the altar. Once centrally located in Christian house churches, the altar gradually lost its place in the worship space, and by the year 500 A.D. was moved against the wall of the apse, where it eventually served as a supporting structure for beautifully adorned and gilded tabernacles.

Originally designed to house the reserved Eucharist for the sick and dying, the tabernacle soon became a focal point of the worship space. Often inlaid with jewels and surrounded by stunning images of cherubs and saints, the prominence given to the tabernacle in the worship space symbolized an important shift in eucharistic theology that occurred in the church by the Middle Ages. This shift placed more emphasis on the static presence of Christ in the consecrated species than on the living presence of Christ in the worshiping assembly. To designate the importance of the tabernacle, a special area was created. This area, called the sanctuary, was reserved for the tabernacle, the ordained clergy, and members of the royal family, those deemed worthy to be in the presence of God. A railing now separated the faithful from the eucharistic action of the table. This succeeded not only in dividing the worship space in half but also, more important, contributed to an era of ecclesial imbalance between the two living realities of the church: namely the perceived holiness of the ordained and the perceived unworthiness of the laity. The faithful, now considered unworthy and physically separated from the action of the liturgy, focused on the *reserved* Eucharist as an object of worship and adoration. They also began to turn to the saints of their times, especially the Blessed Virgin Mary, in search of spiritual fulfillment. Gradually, the focus of the Mass for the gathered worshipers shifted to individual prayer rather than communal prayer. The use of Latin as the language of liturgical prayer, a language unknown to the laity in the pews, contributed to the practice of personal prayer and devotions during the liturgy. This further estranged the faithful from the liturgical action, but conferred awe and mystery on the liturgy.

During the Middle Ages, construction continued on larger and more impressive church structures. These gothic cathedrals had cavernous and majestic interiors with ornately painted ceilings and golden domes, towering high above those who came to pray. In the end larger and more stately structures to house the presence of God produced tragic results, for the primacy of the gathered assembly at worship was all but lost in the midst of these majestic spaces.

Long, narrow aisles and rows of seating barely accommodated the faithful and placed even more emphasis on the actions of the ordained. Throughout the interior of the buildings, beautiful artistic renderings, enormous crucifixes, and imposing tabernacles provided the faithful with foci for their private prayer during the liturgy. Robert Duggan explains, "The sense of religious mystery, which permeated the cavernous interiors of grand old churches while the priest offered the Holy Sacrifice of the Mass, provided a contact with God" (9). The faithful found contentment in the beautiful surroundings of the church interior and their passive role at liturgy. The overwhelming beauty and majesty of these grand churches served to silence the assembly, rather than invite them into participation. Over the course of time, the term *church* became synonymous with sacred spaces built of mortar and stone, rather than the living reality of the gathered Body of Christ. The worshiping assembly gradually became silent spectators affixed on private prayer and personal salvation. This was the role of the laity at worship until the eve of the Second Vatican Council.

> In the reform and promotion of the liturgy, this full and active participation by all the people is the aim to be considered above all else (CSL 14).

The documents that emanated from the Second Vatican Council heralded an enormous shift in the patterns of worship, which requires the full, conscious, and active participation of the faith community in the liturgical celebration.

Change is difficult for all of us. We are creatures of habit, and there is a reassuring sense of order to the daily rituals of ordinary life. In 1963, when the Second Vatican Council initiated the reforms in the Roman Catholic liturgy, overnight familiar ways gave way to the unfamiliar. While many perceived these changes as exciting and challenging to their faith life, others viewed them with trepidation, calling into question abandonment of time-honored practices esteemed for centuries by devout Roman Catholics. These liturgical reforms lie at the heart of many heated discussions around the renewed liturgy. The liturgical changes often met with great resistance and consternation due in part to a lack of proper preparation, catechesis, and pastoral sensitivity in the institution of the changes. Neither the clergy nor the new lay leadership was equipped to properly prepare the faithful for the changes of the reformed liturgy. As a result, many seemed superficial and arbitrary to the faithful.

In an attempt to promote active participation of the whole assembly in liturgical worship, physical changes were made to the worship space. Altar tables were repositioned to face the assembly. The priest now celebrated liturgy facing the gathered community. Communion railings were disassembled, encouraging access of the laity to the sanctuary. The hurried frenzy of uncatechized changes to the sacred space and liturgical practices resulted in many people harboring hurt feelings and longing for the "good old days." Art historian Marchita Mauck writes that these post–Vatican II changes left many Catholics with the same feeling that St. Jerome must have felt "when barbarians laid waste to the city of Rome, that the world as we had known it was no more" (153). We may chuckle at this comparison, but a large number of practicing Catholics today still carry the wounds from those initial days of reform. Before these faithful can truly enter into active participation of the renewed liturgy, their issues require pastoral attention and sensitivity. Today we are finding that many younger Catholics also long for the "good old days." This nostalgia, evidenced in both young and old alike, points to a reality that places emphasis on physical aspects of the worship building and spiritual passivity rather than the full, conscious participation of the worshiping community. If our goal is to move the faithful toward full, conscious, and active participation in the public worship of the church, our faithful must first reclaim their baptismal identity as members of the Body of Christ.

We are initiated into the community of believers and called to active participation in the liturgical mysteries of the church through the life-giving baptismal waters. The Christian journey that begins at the font leads to the ambo, where the living word of God proclaimed in our midst calls us to discipleship. Inspired by the word, our Christian journey ultimately leads us to the table of the Lord, where we are invited to transformation — to become more like Christ and to begin our Christian mission. Our communal worship is an encounter with the living Christ. Through the primary symbols of worship, we experience God's unconditional gift of love, reconciliation, and transformation. Here in this sacred place, we are given the eyes to see and the ears to hear that which enables us to walk the journey with others in a world that is shattered and broken.

As we look to the future, let us revere the past, celebrate the present, and look to the future as a faith community united through the waters of baptism as we open ourselves to God's grace and transformation through the primary symbols of worship.

Discussion Questions

1. What are your memories or experiences of the liturgical reforms of the Second Vatican Council?

2. What experiences of church are evoked when you hear the phrase "the good old days"?

3. What is your experience of the word "church"? What does this word evoke?

4. How can we help our worshiping assemblies reclaim their identity as church? as active liturgical participants?

Meditation (for use with groups)

Select a time when your church building will be open for quiet prayer and reflection. If possible, try to sit close to the sanctuary for this spiritual exercise. As you sit in the pew, close your eyes and try to imagine how the early Christian communities celebrated Eucharist.

- Imagine the joy and excitement the first Christians experienced as they eagerly gathered around the table of the Lord.

- Imagine the aroma of freshly baked bread and the sweet bouquet of sun-ripened crushed grapes that fill the air of this communal meal setting.

- Reflect on the words of Jesus:

"Take and eat; this is my body" (Mt 26:26).

"Take and drink, this is the cup of my blood.
Do this in remembrance of me" (1 Cor 11:25).

- Envision that the bread is now broken apart, and a piece is placed in your hand. As you partake of this sacred meal, the cup passes around the table for you to drink.

- Am I bread for others? How do I pour myself out in service to my family? my friends? the world?

- What does it mean to drink from the cup of Christ?

- Stay with this image awhile. Let it soak into your imagination.

- Now, slowly open your eyes and look around you. What feelings does this sacred place evoke?

- What images do the waters of the font bring to mind?

- In what ways does the proclaimed word summon me to transformation, self-sacrifice, and mission?

- How am I to become the Body and Blood of Christ in the world?
- Am I aware of the gathered community?
- Is my liturgical experience passive or active? Why?

Chapter Two

The Waters of Baptism: Doorway to New Life and Call to Community

The first time I witnessed a baptism by immersion, the richness of the profound mystery unfolding before my eyes overwhelmed me. My heart ached with sadness, for I knew my own experience of baptism was nothing like this. Born and raised a Catholic, my personal experiences of this life-giving ritual were that of the "christening" of babies. For me, the word *baptism* evoked imagery of water trickling over a baby's forehead and a scant chrism anointing with a cotton ball. These vignettes of the celebration of baptism were the sum of my illustrated religious experience of this sacrament throughout the years.

On that Easter Vigil night, as I witnessed the rebirth of God's holy people coming to the waters of life, my entire perception of baptism changed. I watched with joy as each candidate was immersed into the life-giving baptismal waters of the font, and I witnessed the delight in every face of those receiving new life. Moreover, I experienced the spontaneous rejoicing of the assembly, which sang a glorious "Alleluia!" to welcome each new member into the community. At that moment, the newly baptized women, men, and children, wrapped in towels and lovingly embraced by the celebrant, were aglow with the light of Christ, radiant in the joy of the Spirit, and one with the gathered assembly of believers. As the priest anointed the neophytes with oil, the fragrance of chrism hung in the air, and the grace of this sacrament was upon the entire gathered community. Truly, this was baptism as I never experienced it! The liturgical rituals of the bath of rebirth, the gift of the illumination of Christ, and the chrismation seal of the Spirit deeply touched my heart and awakened my baptismal identity as priest, prophet, and king. The spiritual rebirth that I took for granted now became the doorway to my membership in the living Body of Christ: a life reborn of water and the Spirit, a life whose journey leads me from the life-giving waters of the font to the nourishment of word and sacrament and ultimately to mission into the world.

Baptism: The Building Block of Community

> Baptism is the sacrament by which its recipients are incorporated into the Church and are built up together in the Spirit into a house where God lives (see Eph 2:22), into a holy nation and a royal priesthood (see 1 Pet 2:9). Baptism is a sacramental bond of unity linking all who have been signed by it (see UR 22) (RCIA GI 4).

Through the sacrament of baptism, we receive a share in the common community of believers, and as such we all share in the mission of Jesus Christ.

> Having become a member of the Church, the person baptized belongs no longer to himself, but to him who died and rose for us (CCC 1269; see also 1 Cor 6:19 and 2 Cor 5:15).

> Baptism therefore constitutes *the sacramental bond of unity* existing among all who through it are reborn (CCC 1271, quoting UR 22§2).

In the days before the council, the widely accepted reason for baptism was the remission of original sin. Today the church teaches that not only do the life-giving waters of baptism wash away all sin, but also that "baptism makes us members of the Body of Christ: 'Therefore ... we are members one of another' (Eph 4:25). Baptism incorporates us *into the Church*" (CCC 1267). The sacrament of baptism reinforces our call to be one with the community of believers:

> The preparation for baptism and Christian instruction are both of vital concern to God's people, the Church, which hands on and nourishes the faith received from the apostles. Through the ministry of the Church, adults are called to the Gospel by the Holy Spirit and infants are baptized in the faith of the Church and brought up in that faith. ... In the actual celebration, **the people of God ... should take an active part** [emphasis added]. Thus they will show their common faith and the shared joy with which the newly baptized are received into the community of the Church (RCIA GI 7).

Clearly, the sacramental bond of baptism that unites all believers into the *one* living Body of Christ also invites the *entire* living Body of Christ to take an active part in the celebration. This is difficult to achieve if the sacrament of baptism is routinely celebrated privately, outside the liturgical celebration of Sunday Mass. While some may argue that Sunday afternoon baptismal celebrations are communal in nature because families and friends are gathered, the faith communities with which these families regularly worship are not present to experience the glory of new life and to welcome that new life into the faith community. In recent years many parishes have made a concerted effort to celebrate infant baptisms at Sunday Eucharist. These sacramental liturgies offer the gathered community a chance to witness the baptism of new members into the community and provide an opportunity for the community to reflect on their own baptismal promises, their call to community, and to active participation.

The experience of baptism should be abundant; our sacramental symbols must be broken open and used lavishly. Employing the ritual of pouring or immersion, the baptismal water should be plentiful to fully express the reality of the new life received in baptism:

> Water is the key symbol of baptism and the focal point of the font. In this water believers die to sin and are reborn to new life in Christ (BLS 68).

Citing water as the primary symbol of the sacrament of baptism may seem rather obvious, but if one's previous experience of baptism consisted of a small trickle of water from a gilded shell, perhaps it is time to take a closer look at what the symbol of the living water means to the Christian life. Oil should also be lavishly administered through the gift of touch rather than a chrismation, neatly sealed using a sterile cotton ball.

The following guidelines assist faith communities in experiencing the fullness of baptism:

1. One font for baptism of both infants and adults symbolizes the one faith and one baptism that all Christians share.

2. The abundant use of water for the baptism of adults and infants more fully expresses the theology of baptism of dying and rising to a new life in Christ, whether by immersion or infusion (pouring).

3. Baptism is a sacrament of the whole church and particularly of the local parish community, and it should be administered in the presence of the whole community.

4. Whenever the faith community blesses themselves with holy water, they recall their own baptism and baptismal promises.

Discussion Questions

1. How does your faith community celebrate the sacrament of baptism?

2. What can you do to help the faithful envision baptism as the sacrament of entry?

3. In what ways can we help our assemblies make the connection between baptism and Eucharist?

Breaking Open the Symbols of Baptism (for use with small groups)

If possible, do this spiritual exercise around the baptismal font. If that is not possible, fill a large glass bowl with holy water and place it near the entrance of the sacred space. Everyone present should encircle the living water. Also light the Easter candle and place it near the source of water.

Additional items needed: a table, tablecloth, hand towel, small glass bowl, jar of olive oil, and taper candles for each person present.

Prayer Leader: My dear friends,
We come together this day to give thanks and praise
To God for the gift of our baptism.
Through the font of living waters,
We have been reborn of water and Spirit.
May the Lord renew us in Spirit,
That we may bring the light of Christ to all people.
We ask this through Christ our Lord. Amen.

Scripture Reading: Matthew 3:13–17

Reflective Silence

Invite all present to light their candles from the Easter candle.

Renewal of Baptismal Vows

Prayer Leader: With grateful hearts, let us renew our baptismal promises together:
Do you reject Satan?

All: I do.

Prayer Leader: And all his works?

All: I do.

Prayer Leader: And all his empty promises?

All: I do.

Prayer Leader: Do you believe in God the Father Almighty, creator of heaven and earth?

All: I do.

Prayer Leader: Do you believe in Jesus Christ, his only Son, our Lord,
Who was crucified, died, and was buried,
Rose from the dead,
And is now seated at the right hand of the Father?

All: I do.

Prayer Leader: Do you believe in the Holy Spirit,
The holy catholic church,
The communion of saints,
The forgiveness of sins, the resurrection
Of the body, and life everlasting?

All: I do.

Prayer Leader: God, the all-powerful Father of our Lord Jesus Christ,
Gave us a new birth by water and
The Holy Spirit and forgives all our sins.
May God also keep us faithful to our Lord
Jesus Christ forever and ever. Amen.

Extinguish candles.

Blessing with Holy Water

Prayer Leader: As members of the one Body of Christ,
 Let us be grateful to God for the gift of faith,
 Entrusted to us through these life-giving waters.

Invite all to dip their hands into the water and bless themselves.

A brief period of silent thanksgiving follows.

(Instrumental music)

Anointing with Oil

Prayer Leader: Sealed with the gift of the Holy Spirit
 On the day of our baptism, may this oil be a reminder
 Of our baptismal anointing as priest, prophet, and king.

The prayer leader pours oil into the glass bowl and anoints the hands of each person, making the sign of the cross.

A short period of reflective silence follows.

(Instrumental music)

Closing Prayer

Prayer Leader: Let us pray. Lord,
 We thank you for the gift of new life
 Given to us through the sacrament of baptism.
 May our lives, reborn of water and spirit,
 Lead us to the one table of the Lord,
 Who lives and reigns with you and the Holy Spirit,
 One God forever and ever. Amen.

Chapter Three

The Ambo: Altar of the Living Word

> The two parts that ... go to make up the Mass, namely, the liturgy of the word and the liturgy of the eucharist, are so closely connected with each other that they form but one single act of worship (CSL 56).

In spite of the Second Vatican Council's restoration of the prominence of the word in the renewed liturgy, many still place greater importance on the Liturgy of the Eucharist than on the Liturgy of the Word. Sunday after Sunday, good and faithful people routinely arrive late at Mass, often during or even after the readings, and some even arrive just before the communion procession. This practice is a residual of the era just prior to the liturgical reforms of the Second Vatican Council. In those days people considered the offertory, consecration, and priest's communion the primary parts of the Mass. If the faithful were present for those three elements, they fulfilled their Sunday obligation. Unfortunately, this preconciliar ecclesiology placed emphasis on the Eucharist and greatly diminished the importance of the word of God in the liturgical life of the church.

Aware of the importance of sacred Scripture to the faith life of all Christians, the bishops of the Second Vatican Council restored the word of God to its rightful and prominent role in liturgical celebrations: "The intimate connection between the liturgy of the word and the liturgy of the Eucharist in the Mass should prompt the faithful to be present right from the beginning of the celebration" (LM 48). Drawing from the wisdom and prophecy of the Old Testament, the moral teachings of the New Testament, and the four Gospels of Jesus Christ, sacred Scriptures tells our faith story, instructs us, and transforms us to live the life God intends. We encounter Christ not only in the Eucharist, but also in the Scriptures proclaimed in our midst. The church declares that in the liturgy, Christ is present in four ways: *in the word as it is proclaimed, in the minister presiding, in the gathered assembly, and most especially in the consecrated elements of bread and wine* (see CSL 7). Apparently, from liturgical practices on the part of the faithful, this fourfold expression of Christ's presence is not yet fully realized. Noted theologian and liturgical scholar Edward Foley comments, "I believe most Roman Catholics hold that Christ is 100% present in the consecrated elements ... but when it comes to the word, maybe 60%, the presider maybe 30% ... and the assembly ... well, set your own number ("Become What You Eat" 13).

The Word of God

> In the beginning was the Word,
>   and the Word was with God,
>   and the Word was God (John 1:1).

The *spoken* word comes to life when heard by the human ear. As baptized members of the assembly, we are called to be active listeners, not passive readers. "In the liturgy of the word, the congregation of Christ's faithful ... receives from God the word of his covenant through the faith that comes by hearing" (LM 45). Sacred Scripture is the story of God interacting with God's holy people throughout salvation history. It is our story of salvation, and it is a story to which we are called to listen with open hearts so the word may take root in our being. "The word of God reverently received moves the heart and its desires toward conversion and toward a life resplendent with both individual and community faith" (LM 47).

The question often asked is *"What difference does it make if I read the Scriptures at home or listen to them proclaimed during the liturgy?"* The answer is simple: Reading the Bible at home is a marvelous way to enrich one's spiritual life. However, the Scriptures verbally proclaimed in the presence of the gathered assembly breathe life into the written words. The life breath of the Spirit gives power to the spoken word, which converts our hearts and sets them ablaze with the love of God and neighbor. The church teaches that "in the liturgy God is speaking to his people" (CSL 33), opening up to them the mystery of redemption and salvation, and nourishing their spirit; Christ is present to the faithful through his own word. The risen Christ is therefore present in the spoken word, using the voice of the reader and homilist to speak to those gathered in his name. "All the faithful without exception must therefore always be ready to listen gladly to God's word" (LM 47). "The word of God constantly proclaimed in the Liturgy is always, then, a living and effective word" (LM 4), which has the power to teach us, inspire us, and transform our lives as we journey together to the one table of the Lord.

The Ambo: The Altar of God's Word

The ambo is a symbol of God's presence in the word proclaimed. It is a sacred place where God encounters God's holy people through the spoken word. Reserved for proclaiming the readings of the day, the responsorial psalm, the Easter proclamation, the general intercessions, and the homily, it is not a place for use by the song leader, commentator, cantor, or any other casual speaker (see LM 33). "Here the Christian community encounters the Living Lord in the word of God and prepares itself for the 'breaking of the bread' and the mission to live the word that will be proclaimed" (BLS 61).

The faithful, nourished by God's word and the Eucharist, grow in wisdom and holiness. The word reveals our covenant with God, and the everlasting covenant is renewed through the Eucharist (see LM 10). This intimate relationship between the ambo and the altar, between the Liturgy of the Word and the Liturgy of the Eucharist, invites the faithful to actively offer "one single act of divine worship" (LM 10), a single act that will "bring them continuous growth in the spiritual life and draw them more deeply into the mystery which is celebrated" (LM 45).

Discussion Questions

1. Is the ambo used only for the proclamation of the word? Does it bear a resemblance to the table of the Eucharist?

2. As ministers of the assembly, we are called to be active listeners of the word of God. How does one cultivate the skill of active listening? Is there silence between readings?

3. How does ancient Scripture speak to the Christian of the twenty-first century?

4. Does the quality of the liturgical books (lectionary and Gospels) reflect the importance of the living word of God? How do we demonstrate reverence and respect for these sacred books?

5. What type of lector formation program does your parish have? Does a regularly scheduled ongoing spiritual renewal program for lectors exist?

6. The spirituality of a lector is rooted in sacred Scripture. In what ways should proclaimers of the word prepare for their ministry?

Guided Meditation (for an individual or group)

If possible, gather near the ambo for this meditation.

Begin by relaxing your body and mind. Find a comfortable place to sit. Invoke the Holy Spirit to help you fully give yourself to the moment.

Prayer

> Lord, send your Spirit into my heart,
> That I may be open to receiving your life-giving word.
> Let this word, rich as it is, nourish my heart, increase my faith, and lead me to your heavenly banquet.
> We ask this through Christ our Lord. Amen.

Suggested Scriptures:

Nehemiah 8:2–4,5–6,8–10; or Luke 4:14–21

As the Scripture passage is read, focus your complete attention on the reader. The body language, eye contact, and facial expression of the reader can help draw you into the activity of listening.

Responsorial Psalm: Psalm 19:8–10

> Lord, you have the words of everlasting life.
>
> **R: Lord, you have the words of everlasting life.**
>
> The law of the Lord is perfect,
> Refreshing the soul.
> The decree of the Lord is trustworthy,
> Giving wisdom to the simple.
>
> **R: Lord, you have the words of everlasting life.**
>
> The precepts of the Lord are right,
> Rejoicing the heart.

The command of the Lord is clear,
Enlightening the eye.

R: Lord, you have the words of everlasting life.

The fear of the Lord is pure,
Enduring forever.
The ordinances of the Lord are true,
All of them just.

R: Lord, you have the words of everlasting life.

They are more precious than gold,
Than a heap of purest gold;
Sweeter also than syrup
Or honey from the comb.

R: Lord, you have the words of everlasting life.

Faith Sharing

Sacred Scripture infuses us with the presence of the incarnate Christ.

As you listen to the Scripture proclaimed, does a particular word or image touch your heart? Spend a few moments to reflect on how the word of God speaks to you today.

Share your thoughts with the person next to you, and compare your insights with that of your neighbor. Are your insights the same? Or, because your life experiences are different, does this Scripture reading speak to the heart of another in a way different than yours?

Chapter Four

The Altar: Table of Transformation

> At the Last Supper Christ instituted the Paschal Sacrifice and banquet by which the Sacrifice of the Cross is continuously made present in the Church whenever the priest, representing Christ the Lord, carries out what the Lord himself did and handed over to his disciples to be done in his memory (GIRM 72).

Baptized into the faith of the church, we are invited to the divine banquet. Each time we begin our journey to the table, we are called to community, to conversion, to participation, and to communion with the Lord and one another.

The Eucharistic Prayer

> Now the center and summit of the entire celebration begins: namely, the Eucharistic Prayer, that is, the prayer of thanksgiving and sanctification. The priest invites the people to lift up their hearts to the Lord in prayer and thanksgiving; he unites the congregation with himself in the prayer that he addresses in the name of the entire community to God the Father through Jesus Christ. ... The meaning of the Prayer is that the entire congregation of the faithful should join itself with Christ in confessing the great deeds of God and in the offering of Sacrifice (GIRM 78).

How many U.S. Catholics truly experience the eucharistic prayer as the "center and summit" of the liturgical celebration? More often, this prayer, which lies at the heart of our liturgical celebration, leads the faithful not into thanksgiving and sanctification but rather into an interlude of spiritual boredom culminating with an individual act of eucharistic piety.

In the eucharistic prayer, we profess the core of our Roman Catholic faith, namely, that through the invocation of the Holy Spirit and the words of institution, the simple gifts of bread and wine change into the Body and Blood of Christ (see CCC 1353). The consecrated gifts, the acceptable sacrifice, is broken and poured out for all to share. In the eucharistic prayer, the church teaches that not only are the elements of bread and wine the objects of transformation, but so also are the lives of all who gather around the table (see CCC 1368). Baptized into the paschal mystery of Christ, we are called to place our very existence on the altar of sacrifice alongside the gifts of bread and wine. This invitation to unite ourselves to the sacrifice of Christ does not come without consequence; for as we place our own wounded lives on the altar, broken and poured out for others, we enter into the depths of the mystery of the death and resurrection of Jesus Christ. The late Cardinal Bernardin wrote:

> We are called to the Lord's table less for solace than for strength, not so much for comfort as for service. This prayer, then, is prayed not only over the bread and wine, so that they become Christ's body and blood for us to share; it is prayed over the entire assembly so that we may become the dying and rising Christ for the world. Participation in this great prayer of praise, as meal and sacrifice, transforms us. By grace, we more and more become what we pray (17).

The transforming grace that grants us a share in the Body and Blood of Christ and plunges us into the death and resurrection of Christ also summons us into the mission work of the church as the living Body and Blood of Christ.

Called to Transformation and Mission

> What difference does it make if the bread and wine turn into the Body and Blood of Christ, and we don't?

These words, attributed to the late Godfrey Diekmann, OSB, call us to an authentic soul-searching and conversion of the heart, for the divine transformation of the eucharistic celebration should not end with the elements of bread and wine. By the power of the Holy Spirit, we, the living Body of Christ, must also be transformed, or what difference does it make? Roman Catholic tradition teaches us that during the eucharistic prayer, Christ becomes truly and substantially present in the bread and wine through the invocation of the Spirit and the words of consecration. These gifts of bread and wine, the work of human hands and now the Body and Blood of Christ, call us to transformation. We are called to go into the world and become bread to others, to bleed for others, to pour out our lives for others as did Christ. What difference does it make if we piously share in Eucharist week after week, yet remain indifferent to the injustices of our world? What difference does it make if we pray devoutly before God in the blessed sacrament, yet fail to experience the Lord in those we meet each day? What difference does it make if we feast on the Body and Blood of Christ, yet do not pour out the love of Christ for others in our workplaces, homes, and families?

Eucharist is the feast of transformation, and it should inspire us to seek justice and peace for all humankind. It is not intended to be a practice of personal piety but a call to transformation that commissions us for our world mission to courageously proclaim the good news of Jesus Christ for the good of all. Scripture is filled with stories of those whom Jesus loved and for whom he poured out his life: the tax collectors, the prostitutes, the nonbelievers, and the criminals. After an encounter with Christ, they changed; the presence of the living God transformed them. As Roman Catholic Christians, if we truly believe Christ is present in the eucharistic gifts of bread and wine, and if we are to be like those who dined at table with Christ, we must allow the Eucharist to lead us to conversion and transformation. We must allow ourselves to be the Body and Blood of Christ in the world—or what difference does it make?

> *The altar,* around which the Church is gathered in the celebration of the Eucharist, represents the two aspects of the same mystery: the altar of the sacrifice and the table of the Lord (CCC 1383).
>
> It "signifies to the assembly of the faithful one Christ and the one Eucharist of the Church" (BLS 56; RDCA ch. 4, no. 9).

The altar of sacrifice invites us to unite ourselves with the gifts of bread and wine offered to God. As members of the baptized community of believers, we gather around the table of the Lord to feast on the bread of life and to drink from the cup of eternal salvation.

Our Christian journey, which begins at the font of living waters ultimately, leads us to the eucharistic table, where we enter into union with God and one another. At this table, transformed by the Spirit through the bread of life and the cup of salvation, we dare to become nourishment for others in a world that hungers for God.

Discussion Questions

1. How do we experience/participate in the eucharistic prayer?

2. In what ways can we be bread for others?

3. What is implied by the action of drinking from the cup of Christ?

4. What is your experience of the altar table? Is it the focal point of the action of the worshiping community? Is it accessible by all members of the faith community?

5. "The altar is Christ (GIRM 299)" (BLS 56). How should we show reverence and respect for the table of the Lord?

Guided Meditation

If possible, all present should sit around or near the altar.

Prayer Leader: Mindful of the many ways our life is broken and poured out in loving service to our families, our friends, and our coworkers, let us take a moment to quiet our hearts as we listen to the word of God.

Scripture Reading: John 6:53–58

Reflective Silence

Prayer Leader: The altar table is a symbol of Christ, the unblemished lamb who offered himself as a living sacrifice for our sins. Through our baptisms, we are called to share in the one sacrifice of Christ. I now invite you to come forward and symbolically place the gift of yourself on the altar of the Lord.

Each person comes forward, placing his or her hand on the table as they offer the gift of themselves to the Lord in silent prayer. Instrumental music underscores the ritual.

- What are we willing to place on the table?

- What are we willing to let die so we might rise to a new life in communion with Jesus?

After the ritual ends, invite all present to stand.

Prayer Leader: United as one family, let us offer our prayer to God in the words that Jesus gave us:

Our Father …

Gracious God,
As your sons and daughters,
May we be ever mindful of our
Call to renewal, conversion, and transformation.
Pour out your Spirit on us that we may
Share the good news of
Jesus Christ with all people,
As we offer ourselves as bread for others.
We ask this through Christ our Lord. Amen.

At the end of the service, invite all to come forward and reverence the altar.

Chapter Five

The Worshiping Assembly: The Living Body of Christ

Several years ago, as I sat in the back of church during one of our weekly school liturgies, I experienced what many would call an "aha" moment. As I watched the teachers approach the altar table during the Lamb of God, I was suddenly overwhelmed with a sense of community, a sense of being one with them at a profoundly spiritual level. No barriers existed, no walls of division nor isolation came between us. I experienced an intimate spiritual bond with others that I had never before experienced. I've reflected on that moment many times, and no adequate words exist to describe the experience of that particular morning. It opened my heart to the true concept of community, and I recognized the presence of Christ in each of them.

> The assembly, is a radically inclusive body. It embraces all the baptized—the people *and* their ministers, women *and* men, children *and* adults, rich *and* poor, "somebodies" *and* "nobodies," familiar friends *and* struggling strangers, the ordained *and* the non-ordained (Mitchell 9).

This marvelous description of the worshiping gathered assembly is a glimpse of the kingdom of God, where all are welcomed. The challenge is how we blend these diverse individuals from all lifestyles into a worshiping assembly, united as one before the Lord. As daughters and sons of God, we are members of the same family, united in baptism and gathered not as individuals but as members of the living Body of Christ.

> This assembly has come together because its members have been baptized into the one body of Christ and share a common faith. This faith, though rooted in a common baptismal identity, is expressed in ways that extend from the highest levels of personal appropriation and intellectual understanding to the most immature forms of ritualism and

routine. And yet, to a greater or lesser degree, it is faith in Jesus Christ that is common to all the members of a community gathered for Eucharist (FIYH 9).

The church recognizes this essential need for the gathering of God's holy people, not as individuals affixed on their own personal prayer but as one worshiping body united in a common faith; part of the universal Roman Catholic Church. The spiritual bond of baptism that joins all Christians is the foundation for the Second Vatican Council's vision of a gathered assembly:

> In the celebration of Mass the faithful form a holy people, a people whom God has made his own, a royal priesthood, so that they may give thanks to God and offer the spotless Victim not only through the hands of the priest but also together with him, and so that they may learn to offer themselves. They should, moreover, endeavor to make this clear by their deep religious sense and their charity toward brothers and sisters who participate with them in the same celebration.
>
> Thus, they are to shun any appearance of individualism or division, keeping before their eyes that they have only one Father in heaven and accordingly are all brothers and sisters to each other."
>
> Indeed, they form one body, whether by hearing the word of God, or by joining in the prayers and the singing, or above all by the common offering of Sacrifice and by a common partaking at the Lord's table. This unity is beautifully apparent from the gestures and postures observed in common by the faithful (GIRM 95–96).

This vision of the gathered assembly precludes individual prayer and piety, as was the custom in preconciliar days. It is a beautiful image of a gathering of God's holy people, bonded by a common baptism and united before our Father in heaven. There are, however, practical social and cultural issues of inclusivity that continue to hamper the unity of a faith community. These need to be addressed.

- How do we break down the walls of individualism in a society that esteems the rights of the individual?

- How do we overcome prejudices and fears and recognize the face of God in all humanity?

- How do we forgive and ask forgiveness—to reconcile with God's children?

Hospitality and Christian Worship

The art and gift of hospitality is a key element for bringing people together from all walks of life and helping them feel connected with one another. Although the need for hospitality in Christian worship grew out of the council's vision for the gathered assembly, its origins date back to biblical tradition. Abraham had no idea he was entertaining angels when he offered three strangers refreshments in the heat of the desert (see Gen 18:1–5). Nor did the widow at Zarephath know the blessings she would receive by sharing the last of her food with a stranger (see 1 Kings 17:19–24). Yet, the Lord rewarded both acts of kindness and hospitality.

Hospitality is essential to Christian worship because it cultivates a climate in which strangers become friends and friends become like family. It is unrealistic to expect people to form a worshiping community without first extending some form of greeting. Hospitality is a fundamental component to any human social encounter because it provides a welcome and comfortable atmosphere, a sense of belonging. As Christians, we are called to live our baptismal promises, to seek the face of Christ in the young and the old, the rich and the poor, the "somebodies and the nobodies," and to extend our hands in friendship. The concept of hospitality can sometimes be misunderstood. It isn't meant to be idle chatter between parishioners to catch up on the latest sports score or weather. Hospitality calls for a reverent concern for one another, offering support to those who experience difficult times and welcoming the stranger in our midst. It is the ability to recognize the face of Christ in every person and to respond in a loving and caring manner.

Throughout the centuries of Roman Catholicism, we have been very good about responding to the presence of Christ in the Eucharist, especially in the tabernacle. Why do we find it so difficult to see the divine presence in our brothers and sisters with whom we are united in baptism? If we find it difficult to reverence the presence of Christ in every person, how can we live out the church's vision for a gathered assembly? How can we expect to be church to one another? Hospitality transforms a faith community. It invites strangers to return and makes neighbors feel like family. A faith community that understands hospitality is a community open to transformation and renewal and will foster warmth, friendship, and acceptance. When people feel comfortable with one another, when the walls of isolation come tumbling down, a faith community is free to embrace openly the call to participation and to work together to build up the kingdom of God.

The Primacy of the Assembly at Worship

> For the aim and object of apostolic works is that all who are made children of God by faith and baptism should come together to praise God in the midst of his Church, to take part in the sacrifice, and to eat the Lord's Supper (CSL 10).

This conciliar statement challenges all baptized believers. It challenges the silent spectators, those devoted to private prayer during the community's liturgical celebration, those who sit behind walls of isolation and loneliness. It challenges the rich and the poor, the "somebodies and the nobodies." It challenges each of us who come together in worship to participate actively in the living words, gestures, and sacrifice of the eucharistic celebration; because the experience of the sacred is found in these actions. We must never forget that liturgy is the work of all the people, not just a few. As we stand before the table of the Lord, we must recognize that we, too, are broken and wounded and call on the transforming power of the Spirit to renew us, for "divine wisdom becomes present to the community through its worship" (Foley, "Minor Exorcisms" 37). If we desire to be people who break open and lavishly use our primary symbols of faith, we must allow these symbols to renew us and call us to participation, for the call to participation is the call to renewal. As people of faith, reborn in water and spirit, we are continually called by God and commissioned in the name of Jesus Christ to go out into the world to be disciples to all nations. The life-giving Spirit, the breath of God, is at work in each of us, transforming us through the primary symbols of worship, renewing the sacred space within.

Discussion Questions

1. What has been your experience of the gathered community at prayer: individuals affixed on their own private prayers or a real sense of communal prayer?

2. We are all called to be one with the Lord and to shun any appearance of individualism or division. In a multicultural community, how can we best achieve this vision?

3. How do we welcome newcomers/visitors to our parish family?

4. In the spirit of Christian hospitality, how do we respond to a parent with a restless child? to someone with a physical disability?

5. Would you invite a stranger who seems alone to sit with you?

6. How serious do we take our responsibility to be people of justice and peace in our community? our families? the world?

Guided Meditation (for use with small groups)

Preferably, do this meditation in the worship space.

Prayer Leader: Creator God,
 Through the waters of baptism,
 We are called and gifted in the image of your Son, Jesus.
 Nourished in word and sacrament,
 May we bring your loving presence
 To a world steeped in the darkness of sin.
 We ask this through Christ our Lord. Amen.

Scripture Reading: Ephesians 4:1–6

Reflective Silence

Faith Sharing

We are one Body, one Spirit in the Lord. As we gather for worship each week, in what ways can we be the Body of Christ, called and gifted, wounded and broken, renewed and transformed?

Prayer Leader: As one family in Christ, let us join hands as we pray in the words our Savior gave us:

Our Father …

Let us now offer one another a sign of the peace of Christ.

Closing Prayer

God of all seasons and time,
From the beginning of creation,
You made us in your image and likeness
And called us to be one with you.
We ask your grace to come upon us.

May all who enter find
Life through the living waters of redemption
And a renewed spirit
Through the grace of reconciliation.

In this sacred place, may we
Gather as one family
Around your heavenly table
To feast on the bread of life
And to drink from the cup of salvation.

And from this holy table,
Renewed in body and spirit,
May we go forth to bring your message
Of peace, justice, and love
To all people for all time.
We ask this through Jesus Christ,
Who is our Savior, yesterday, today, and forever.

Chapter *Six*

The Pilgrim Church: Sacred Space in Transition

Our Roman Catholic identity is embedded in the worship experience of the faith community. These sacramental encounters with the risen Christ do not occur as the result of beautifully adorned and well-appointed church buildings. Rather, our graced experiences of the incarnate one flow from the ritual action of God's holy people engaged in worship. Liturgy is the work of the people. It is the work of the baptized faithful, lay and ordained, people from all walks of life, who gather week after week as one worshiping assembly to *listen,* to *respond,* to give *thanks* and *praise,* to *eat* and *drink,* and to *share* in the mission work of Jesus Christ. These life-giving actions of the church are rooted in the primary symbols of worship.

In this fast-paced and transitional world, it is not always possible to celebrate liturgy in the setting of a parish church building. We are pilgrim people, and thus our worship experience often finds us in temporary and transitional sacred spaces where the living church gathers for prayer. We gather to pray in hospital rooms, homes, offices, and classrooms. We worship at workshops, conferences, retreats, and other events. We celebrate outdoor liturgies in parks and on church property. Mission communities and parishes renovating their sacred spaces worship in basements, parish halls, school cafeterias, and auditoriums for extended periods. Jesus promised, "For where two or three are gathered together in my name, there am I in the midst of them" (Mt 18:20). Claiming these transitional settings as sacred space is a challenge. However, if we keep our hearts focused on our experience of Christ in and through the primary symbols of worship, *where we gather for worship will become secondary to how we worship.*

The previous chapters of this book included an invitation to all believers to break open the primary symbols of worship, namely the font, ambo, altar, and assembly, to discover the ways and means in which these life-giving symbols draw us into full and active participation at liturgical celebrations. This chapter provides resources for claiming sacred spaces of worship in temporary and transitional settings. I have also included a rite of leave-taking (see also *Holy People, Holy Place: Rites for the Church's House* by Thomas G. Simons [Chicago: Liturgy Training Publications, 1998], a comprehensive study of the rites of dedication or renovated places of worship).

Resources for Temporary Worship Settings

The following is a resource for claiming sacred space, and you can use it with small groups in providing meaningful and prayerful liturgies in various and temporary worship settings.

For use in all types of temporary worship settings: classrooms, retreats, outdoor liturgies, conferences, auditoriums, hospital rooms, small group gatherings, and individual homes where the domestic church gathers for prayer. Please keep in mind that the action of God's holy people centers around the primary symbols of worship. You should give prominence to the sacred place of word and sacrament.

Liturgical Items Reflective of Primary Symbols of Worship

- A suitable place where you may proclaim the living word of God (Set this sacred space apart, and use it only for the proclamation of the word.)

- Seating arrangement that reflects an intimate, gathered community at prayer (such as semicircular)

- A chair for the presider or leader of prayer

- Lectionary (book of readings) (If you do not use a bound book, you may make a temporary lectionary with sheets of printed paper placed in a suitable binder. *Avoid individual papers.*)

- A large glass bowl filled with holy water, symbolic of the oneness of the baptized community of faith

Additional Items Needed for Eucharistic Celebrations

- A sturdy table to use for an altar (The table should be in close proximity to the gathered assembly and should also be in direct relationship to the table of the word.)

- A white tablecloth to cover the altar table

- A corporal (white square cloth on which gifts of bread and wine are placed)

- Two lit candles

- Crucifix

- Sacramentary (contains prayers for Mass)

- Chalice/purificator

- Bread, wine, and water

- Additional cups and purificators for assembly

- Printed worship aide for assembly's participation (This should include all music, prayers, and responses needed for the active participation of the worshiping assembly. Depending on the circumstances, worship aides need only include the Scripture citation, *because the living word is proclaimed in the midst of the gathered assembly*.)

Additional Items

- An adequate sound system (depending on size and location of gathering)

- Music (if possible)

- Flowers and plants to enhance the temporary environment

- Fabric appropriate to the color of the liturgical season draped over the ambo and/or near other suitable *primary symbols* of worship (Take great care to ensure that all temporary worship settings offer the faithful a welcoming and inviting environment that is conducive to prayer.)

If possible, it is desirable to begin all liturgies or prayer services with a gathering hymn to unify the assembly of believers.

Leave-Taking Ritual

This ritual is created to assist worshiping communities in making a prayerful transition from their former place of worship to a temporary sacred space where they will gather for worship during the time of renovation or construction.

At the end of the exiting liturgy, the presider may offer these or similar words to the gathered assembly:

> My brothers and sisters in Christ,
> The time has come for us to leave this church building.
>
> As Christians, let us remember that we are the living stones,
> God's holy church,
> A pilgrim people whose hearts will find rest
> In the glorious kingdom of God.
>
> Through the life-giving waters of baptism,
> We became one with Christ
> As we were anointed priest, prophet, and king.
>
> Shaped by the living word of God,
> We gather at table to share in the divine
> Fellowship of Jesus,
> With the hope that we may become his faithful disciples in the world.
>
> In the weeks and months ahead,
> May our voices continue to praise God, and
> May we look forward to the day when we
> Shall return to this renewed and sacred space.
>
> Let us now go forth in the peace of Christ.

The presider invites the assembly to join in procession from the church building to the temporary worship space.

Recessional Hymn

As the music begins, designated members from the assembly may approach the altar and carry in procession those liturgical symbols and vessels that you will use in the temporary worship space:

- The Gospel book
- The sacramentary
- Altar candles
- Chalice/corporal
- Bowl of holy water
- Holy oils
- Paschal candle

All of these symbols are indicative of the primary symbols of worship. These liturgical items are carried in procession behind the processional cross and processional candle bearers. The deacon, presider, and the entire assembly follow in procession behind liturgical symbols. You may carry additional symbols of significance to a particular faith community in procession at this time (for example, a statue of Mary or image of your patron saint). As the pilgrim church enters the temporary worship space, liturgical items are placed in preselected areas symbolic of the sacred spaces reserved for the primary symbols of worship. Presider may then lead assembly in a short prayer of blessing:

Almighty God,
We ask your blessings to come upon the parish family of (*name of parish*)
As we gather in this temporary sacred space.
Here may your word be proclaimed in spirit and in truth.
May our brothers and sisters who gather at your altar table
Be nourished in sacrament by your Body and Blood
And become faithful disciples in the world.
And may the work of our hands give glory
And honor to your holy name both now and forever.
We ask this through Christ our Lord. Amen.

The presider sprinkles the assembly with holy water.
You may sing an appropriate hymn to close this leave-taking ritual.

Bibliography

Liturgical Documents

Built of Living Stones: Art, Architecture, and Worship. Washington, D.C.: United States Conference of Catholic Bishops, 2000.

Catechism of the Catholic Church. St. Paul: The Wanderer Press, 1994.

Constitution on the Sacred Liturgy. In *The Liturgy Documents: A Parish Resource.* 3rd ed. Chicago: Liturgy Training Publications, 1991.

Fulfilled in Your Hearing: The Homily in the Sunday Assembly. In *The Liturgy Documents: A Parish Resource.* 3rd ed. Chicago: Liturgy Training Publications, 1991.

General Instruction of the Roman Missal. 3rd ed. Confirmed for use in the Dioceses of the United States. Washington, D.C.: United States Conference of Catholic Bishops, Inc., 2003.

Lectionary for Mass: Study Edition. Chicago: Liturgy Training Publications, 2002.

Rite of Christian Initiation of Adults. Chicago: Liturgy Training Publications, 1988.

Secondary Sources

Bernardin, Cardinal Joseph. *Guide for the Assembly.* Chicago: Liturgy Training Publications, 1997.

Duggan, Robert D. *Parish Liturgy.* Kansas City, Mo.: Sheed and Ward, 1996.

Foley, Edward. "Become What You Eat: A Mystagogical Reflection on the Communion Rite." *Emmanuel* (January/February 2002).

———. "Minor Exorcisms." *Celebrating the Rites of Christian Initiation: Pastoral Reflections.* Chicago: Liturgy Training Publications, 1992.

Mauck, Marchita B. "Sacred Space for Worship." *Liturgical Ministry* (Fall 1997): 153–159.

Mitchell, Nathan. "The Assembly as Minister." *Assembly* 25.2 (March 1999).

Simons, Thomas G. *Holy People, Holy Place: Rites for the Church's House.* Chicago: Liturgy Training Publications, 1998.